Success~~~
Market Research
in a week

Matthew Housden

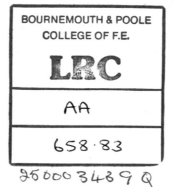
British Library Cataloguing in Publication Data
Author
  Successful market research in a week.
  – (Business in a week)
  I. Title   II. Series
  658.4

ISBN 0 340 56531 4

First published 1992

© 1992 Matthew Housden

Typeset by Multiplex Techniques Ltd, St Mary Cray, Kent
Printed in Hong Kong for the educational publishing division
of Hodder & Stoughton Ltd, Mill Road, Dunton Green,
Sevenoaks, Kent by Colorcraft Ltd.

BIM
British Institute
of Management

The British Institute of Management is the leading
management institute in the UK. It is the driving
force behind the development of professional
management within the public and private sectors.
The Institute embraces all levels of management
from junior managers to chief executives and offers a
unique range of services for all management
disciplines.

If you would like to hear more about the benefits of
individual or corporate membership, please write to

Dept HS
British Institute of Management
Cottingham Road
Corby
Northants NN17 1TT

This series is commissioned by the British Institute
of Management Foundation.

C O N T E N T S

All human activity is based around decisions. To make the right decisions we require information which is pertinent, accurate and timely.

For businesses the same rules apply. Managers make decisions and, to minimise the risks that are an inevitable feature of business practice, these decisions need to be founded on reliable information. Risk will never be eliminated but when presented with the right information, management can use experience and judgement to make the best possible decisions with the least risk.

Providing this information is the broad function of market research.

As business becomes more complex and competitive, the role of information in the decision-making process becomes more important. Profitable activity depends on identifying and fulfilling customer needs in a rapidly changing business evironment. This so-called market-led approach underpins most successful businesses.

Managers need information on who buys a product or service and why, where and when a customer buys. They also need to know who else is supplying the market, what other markets might be targeted and whether technological changes will affect the product.

Market research is therefore not just about markets. It is also about the broader range of influences which affect a company's ability to satisfy its customers' needs profitably.

In this book we will look at the stages involved in carrying out a successful market research project with chapters looking at:

- Market research in business
- Planning market research
- Desk research
- Primary research techniques
- Primary research in practice
- Surveys and data analysis
- The final report

Market research in business

Today, we shall look at the problems market research helps to solve, the opportunities it helps identify and also, the limits of its effectiveness.

Market research has developed several broad divisions. These reflect the range of business problems that face managers.

Research divisions

- Market/customer research
- Promotional research
- Product research
- Distribution research
- Sales research
- Market environment – PEST control

Market research

Today market research and marketing research are interchangable terms. In the past, market research defined a narrower field of enquiry, that of research into the sale of products or services and the customers buying them.

Market research provides the basic knowledge we need about a market. If we are looking at the market for biscuits, for example, research can tell us how many biscuits are sold and how much they are worth.

If we specialise in the manufacture of chocolate biscuits we can find out how many chocolate biscuits are sold and what proportion of the market they account for. This information can be gathered to provide comparisons over time. We can also predict which trends in sales are likely to occur.

Market research will also provide information on our customers. Where do they live? How much do they earn? Are they credit-worthy? It can show us why they prefer one brand of biscuits to another and how much they would pay for them. It can suggest how to improve a product and make it more attractive to current or potential customers.

We can also identify our competitors in the market. We can track our own product's progress against market trends and the progress of our competitors.

Market research will:

- Quantify overall market sizes
- Identify the size of key market sectors
- Show trends over time and provide forecasts
- Provide market and brand shares
- Identify our customers and their buying motivation
- Give information on competitors

Advertising and promotions research

As a major area of expenditure, promotional budgets must be justified. Market research helps measure the success of a campaign against its objectives. Market research is central to the selection of promotional methods and media.

Every product will be supported by some kind of promotional activity. This could be a multi-million pound TV advertising campaign, a stand at a trade fair or simply a press release. What promotional methods does your business use? How are they decided upon? Market research can tell us which promotional method or more importantly, which combination of methods, yields the best and most effective results.

When a communications campaign is being considered, research can tell us which medium is most likely to reach our target audience. It can tell us which TV programmes they watch, which magazines they read and what message is most likely to appeal to them.

Once a campaign strategy has been decided, market research can be used to test it on a small scale before it is launched on a national basis. This testing procedure can reveal any problems in the design of the campaign and associated material. This can save money and often a lot of red faces.

During the promotional campaign, research can be used to establish whether or not our campaign is achieving the results we want. Tracking studies measuring opinion or sales over the course of a campaign help us to control and evaluate the promotion.

Finally the effectiveness of the chosen campaign should be monitored. Effectiveness is measured against the objectives of the campaign. These can be infinitely varied, ranging from creating an awareness of a new product, to reminding the market of our product, to creating a determination in potential customers to buy our product. This means a

variety of research techniques might be called upon to verify
the success or otherwise of any promotional campaign.

Promotional research will:

- Determine the method of promotion
- Enable the testing of copy and campaign
  material testing
- Identify suitable media for our message
- Help determine the effectiveness of
  communications strategy

Product research

Whether the product we are dealing with is a bank account,
a tin of baked beans or a charity, the essence of the product
is that it fulfills a need – the need to keep our money safely,
the need to eat, the desire to give.

As businesses have grown, so too has the distance between
them and their customers. Very few suppliers of goods or

services deal face to face with their clients today. So how can we be sure that our product is fulfilling the need that it was originally intended to satisfy? Maybe our product needs refinement.

Research can show other uses for our product and potential markets for our product which we could profitably develop. If, for example, we are selling our biscuits to the retail trade, we could look at the catering market. If our product is sold in our home country, research might reveal potential export markets.

Research into our customers might show that they have other needs. Perhaps the development of a new product could satisfy these needs. Research can help us test the idea behind the new product before the expensive process of development begins. If the idea is sound, testing prior to launch will iron out any design faults.

Research can help provide an effective assessment of the strengths or weaknesses of our product compared to our competitors' products.

The design and packaging of a product are becoming increasingly important. Design has become a key selling point reinforcing the consumer's image of a product or service. We must ensure that the product can be easily used. We must also make sure that the colours, style and feel of the product match our client's tastes. Market research can help ensure this.

Packaging will reinforce the consumer's idea of the quality of the product. You would not expect to buy an expensive watch wrapped in a plain brown paper bag. This might appear obvious but we need to know that our product's packaging reinforces its unique qualities. It is these qualities which give us the edge on the competition.

Businesses rarely offer the market a single product. Usually a range of products will cover a number of market sectors. Research can show if we would be better focusing our efforts on a particular market sector. Concentrating resources can improve profitability. The overall profitability of a product line might obscure the fact that within the range some products might not be viable and should be withdrawn.

A diversified company with products competing in several different markets might find that resources should be concentrated on a more homogenous product portfolio. Sometimes it is better to be in just the one market where the company performs best. Serving several markets might spread resources too thinly.

Product research will:

- Identify oppportunities for new product development
- Ensure product design enables optimum performance
- Measure product performance against our competitors
- Determine the look and feel of products and packaging
- Assess the contribution of a complementary range of products
- Identify obsolete products

Distribution research

We have seen that, as the business world has become more sophisticated, the distance between a supplier and the end user of the product has become greater.

There are now a variety of 'middlemen' between producers and end users. For example in the grocery business the manufacturer will sell to a wholesaler who will sell to a retailer who then sells to the consumer. Other middlemen include importers, agents, licensees and franchisees.

Research can identify the best channels of distribution for our product and help us find the best agents or retailers for our product.

Look at your own company. What product or service do you market? Is it a mass market product needing wide distribution? Perhaps you are serving an exclusive market and your product is to be available only in up-market stores.

The outlets which stock your product can say a great deal about it.

The need to reach our market is the key to successful business. Distribution research can also show us where to locate warehouses and how to select retail locations.

Distribution research will:

- Determine which distribution method we should use
- Enable the selection of the best middlemen
- Determine the location of outlets

Sales research

A key contact with our market is our sales operation. This can take many forms. We can, for example, use personal selling, mail order or telephone sales.

How do you sell your products? What can you learn from the competition? Have you tried different techniques?

Research can assess and measure the effectiveness of different sales methods against overall trends in the market.

If the company is falling behind, perhaps the reason is that the company is inadequately represented in important new sales outlets. Shifts in the structure of retail sales patterns should be noted and acted upon. For example, petrol stations are becoming important outlets for a wide range of products, from groceries to audio tapes.

Sales research covers all the selling activities of the company. These are usually analysed regionally, the regions being selected for ease of comparison with published information. TV regions are often used. Research can help determine sales regions.

Research can also be carried out on the sales force itself. Are you sure that your sales force is adequately trained? Can they explain the benefits of the products that they are dealing with? Some companies are now using researchers posing as customers to test their sales force.

In addition we can establish if sales force remuneration levels are sufficient to motivate the team and that the levels of commission are correct.

Sales research will:

- Measure the effectiveness of sales methods
- Evaluate alternative or new methods of selling
- Help establish sales territories
- Determine the frequency of sales calls
- Account for regional variations in sales
- Determine remuneration, control and training

Market environment

The manager of a business needs to know more than who is buying the company's products. Other external influences may affect the company's ability to trade profitably. These are usefully remembered by the term PEST control. PEST refers to:

Political influences: a change of government or party policy can obviously affect trading conditions, for example cutting or raising taxes. Of increasing importance is the influence of the European parliament on business.

Economic influences: the economic climate within which a business operates will obviously affect it. Economic analyses can be carried out at the local, national and international level. Short, medium and long range economic forecasting underpins business plans.

Social influences: demographic changes such as the baby boom in the 1960s have a profound effect on a company's business. National culture and morality will influence the way a company markets its products. Companies should be aware of social trends that may influence the market. National governments provide this data.

Technical influences: innovation will also affect the company's business. A look at new patents can help to identify possible threat. For example, the makers of carbon paper would have been interested to know of the patenting of the photocopier.

Market research limitations

As we have seen, market research can help us to deal with a wide range of business decisions. However, market research will only reduce risk, never eliminate it. There is always a degree of uncertainty surrounding business decisions. Even if it were possible, it would be impractical for businesses to gather all the information needed to create conditions of certainty.

Even if we could gather all available information pertinent to a problem, our ultimate decision depends upon our correct interpretation and analysis of this information.

Market research helps the decision-making process but by no means replaces it. Research helps management to prioritise decisions and reduces the number of factors to be considered. Decisions will still need to be made, drawing on the experience and judgement of management.

Limitations are also imposed on research by time and budget constraints.

Summary

Today we saw how market research can be used to help to solve business problems and identify opportunities. We have identified the key areas of market research.

We have also looked at the limitations of the discipline. Awareness of these limitations will help us to produce the objective information we need. However, the practical considerations of timing and budget can also affect the quality of the information we generate.

Successful business management in an increasingly complex environment depends on good decisions. Good decisions depend upon good information. Market research helps to provide this information.

We have seen that market research plays a crucial role in the business decision making process. At its heart lies the need to reduce risks involved in solving business problems and exploiting business opportunities.

Tomorrow we will begin to examine the practice of market research.

Planning market research

Today we shall look at how market research is carried out.

Elements of market research
- The research plan
- Developing a brief
- In-house or external?
- Selecting an agency
- Costing research
- Assessing a proposal

The research plan

This model shows the structure and process of a research plan.

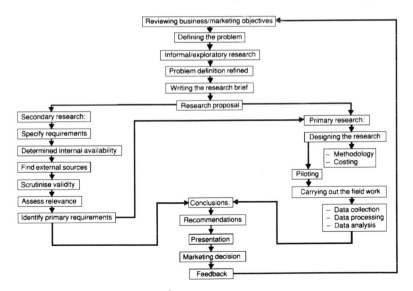

Developing a brief

The importance of a concise and accurate brief cannot be underestimated. Even if the research is small scale and carried out personally or in-house, it is important to have a clear statement of what is expected, by when and at what price. If the research is to be carried out by an external agency, the brief becomes a key document.

The creation of the brief involves the first five stages of the research plan.

Reviewing marketing objectives
Market research is not an end in itself. Market research provides a service. Its life is created by the managers who use the information it provides.

Market research is determined by the marketing aims of a company and its management.

Market research projects therefore will be designed to enhance management decisions. These are made within the confines of the overall business plan. Market research will support the following decision making structure:

- Where are we?
- Where do we want to be?
- How are we going to get there?
- How do we ensure that we arrive?

What are your company's business objectives? How can research help achieve them?

It is important to realise that marketing objectives are not the same as research objectives. A marketing objective might be to enter a new market by a certain date. The research objective might be to establish patterns of buyer behaviour within that market. This analysis will help management make the market entry decision.

The key point to consider is the relationship between market research, marketing and the strategic goals of the company. We should ask the following questions: Is the research indispensable? Can we achieve the company's objectives without expensive market research?

Defining the problem
We have seen that market research covers the complete range of business activities. A perfect situation would be where manageable and relevant information about all these areas was immediately available to managers at all times. Of

course this never happens. The cost of gathering and storing information is prohibitive.

Identification of marketing problems provides a focus for the research project and creates a specific information requirement. Problems must be stated as clearly and specifically as possible. Recognising a problem is half-way to solving it.

In defining the problem and framing the solution we must:

- Involve all interested parties
- Establish measures of success
- Obtain an internal consensus

Informal/exploratory research
This area of the plan is often combined with the more formal and structured use of secondary research. It is important as a separate stage in the plan because it can help us to:

- Learn about unfamiliar markets
- Assess supplementary information
- Build a level of knowledge to communicate to third parties, for example, a research agency.
- Develop new ideas and new angles about a problem

Refining the problem definition
Informal research creates fertile ground for information that might previously have been discarded. It can be supported by telephone calls to key contacts or other personnel or

contacts in the industry, so start to build your own network of industry contacts.

Discussion with other members of the project team will further hone down our information requirements. At this stage, the definition of the problem is changing and becoming sharper as we develop our understanding. Ultimately we create a problem definition which provides the focus for the following stages of the research plan.

Writing the brief
Once the above procedure has been carried out we can see that it is a fairly easy task to put together a research brief.

Contents of the brief
- Company history and background
- The commissioning dept's role in the company
- The history of the problem
- The objectives of the research
- Ideas on research methodology
- Time limits for:
  - submitting the proposal
  - submitting stages of the report
  - presentation of the final report
- Instructions about presentation:
  - how is the final report to be presented?
  - how many copies of the report will be needed?
- The requirements of confidentiality
- A date for discussing the brief in person

If appointing a third party, for example, an internal research department or an external agency, it is not advisable to include a statement of budget at this stage.

Price against quality will be a key determinant in final selection of methodology or agency. At this time an indication of a broad price range should suffice.

In any case, if the problem has been adequately assessed in terms of value versus cost of data, all quotes presented should fall within a relatively narrow band.

In-house or external?

Whether to carry out research in-house or externally is an important decision and several factors should be considered.

Resources
Do we have the resources to undertake a substantial survey? These include:

- Computer processing
- Languages
- Research experience
- Statistical expertise
- Access to a field force

Objectivity
An external agency might bring a higher degree of objectivity to the study. An agency is free to be reasonably critical of in-house practices without fear of career repercussions.

Price
Many companies appear to be put off using external agencies because of the cost they believe is involved. Often, agencies will be no more expensive than using the in-house research department or other members of staff.

Experience
Agencies have established efficient systems for research and certain agencies will specialise in certain industries.

Personnel
In-house staff involved in research are not carrying out other duties.

Confidentiality
Agencies guarantee confidentiality but once the research is in the public domain it has more chance of being talked about. This can be particularly damaging if, for example, conducting an aquisition study.

Conflict of interest
Are other agency clients in competition with us? Maybe they
pay the agency more than we do.

Knowledge of product or service
Is our product highly specialised? Will we have to foot the
bill for the research company's learning process?

Selecting an agency

So how do we go about selecting our agencies? Well, there
are two selection procedures to go through. One involves
choosing those agencies who will receive our briefing
document. The other involves the final selection and
appointment of one of these agencies. We can find the
names of suitable companies in a number of ways:

- The trade press or our trade association might have
  contacts with research companies that we could
  approach.
- Using directories. The Market Research Society in the
  UK provides a list of companies providing research
  services. This gives details of agency size and details
  of any specialist areas that they cover.
- Contacts in the trade may have experience of relevant
  research agencies. Their comments would certainly
  flesh out the often misleading descriptions in any
  directory.

There are a number of criteria to consider when selecting a
short-list of up to three companies from those we have
identified.

Criteria checklist

- Is the company a member of a professional body?
- What is its reputation?
- Have we used them before?
- Were we happy with the results?
- Do they have a conflict of interest?

Make a list of the agencies your company could use. Keep the file up to date.

Costing research

Market research is an expensive commodity. The cost of a failed product launch, however, can be greater. It is vital that companies and their agencies have an appreciation of the ultimate value of the research. This can be set off against the cost of gathering, processing and presenting the information.

Often the decision as to whether to carry out research is made subjectively. The estimated costs are presented and a manager will make a decision to go ahead based largely on a 'feel' for the exercise. This introduces the element of risk that research is attempting to eliminate.

Some projects will be harder to assess than others. It is important that business objectives are quantified either financially or by time.

If our objective is to launch a new biscuit, the size of the market could be evaluated. Our forecast market share will give a basic indicator of expected revenue from this new biscuit. We can then make a more reliable assessment of our market research budget.

The cost of research will vary according to the objectives of the research and its design. For the cost conscious manager the temptation to go for the cheapest option will always exist. It should be remembered that you will only get what you pay for. We must choose a research solution that will solve the defined problem, with one eye on the anticipated returns. The greater the uncertainty about the potential gain, the greater the need for research.

Assessing a proposal

Once the short list has been chosen, and we have presented and discussed the brief, the agency should respond with a proposal for the project. Companies should not usually charge for the presentation of a proposal.

The structure of the proposal might vary but should contain the following elements:

- Background to the problem
- Research objectives
- Planned use of the research
- The information required
- A methodology:
  - sample size
  - techniques
  - field workers
    - number
    - quality control
  - the questionnaire
  - data processing
- A full timetable:
  - when questionnaires will be produced
  - when field work will begin
  - when raw data will be processed
  - the number and nature of progress reviews
  - the date of presentation of any interim reports
  - the date of the final presentation
- The CVs of key personnel
- Details of the presentation of the report:
  - summarised report contents page
  - number of copies
  - type of binding
  - the use of graphics, video etc.
  - the nature and date of any personal presentation
- The cost of the report:
  - are expenses included?
  - what about VAT?
  - how long is the quote valid?

When assessing the agency's proposal, look for the following:

- Have they stuck to or improved the brief?
- Is it cost-effective? Will it fulfill objectives?
- Is their approach creative?
- Does the proposal cover all eventualities? Is it vague?
- Are the personnel experienced?
- Do they fully understand our requirements?
- Can we work with them? Does it feel right?
- How important are we as clients?
- Is the work well controlled?

Summary

Today we have looked at the research plan. We have seen that there is a systematic process we should go through in developing a market research project.

We have seen that the objectives of a market research project are very different from the overall business objectives of the company but that they are inevitably linked.

We have discussed how a research brief is put together and the importance of considering the value of information against the cost of obtaining it.

We can see that the purpose of providing a research brief is to:

- Ensure common understanding internally and with the agency
- Clarify objectives and narrow the problem definition
- Focus research design on these objectives
- Enable the effective comparison of different proposals
- Record formally research goals against which performance can be assessed

We have discussed the selection of agencies and stressed the importance of developing a close working relationship with them. The proposal selected should:

- Present a creative solution to the research problem
- Address every possible eventuality
- Be clearly written
- Be cost effective

Tomorrow we will begin to look at the various research techniques we can use.

Desk research

Today we shall look at the published sources of information which are available to the researcher. These are known as secondary sources.

- Internal sources
- External sources inside the UK
- External sources outside the UK

Secondary vs. primary research

Desk research refers to all research work conducted using secondary sources. It differs from primary research in that data worked on will have already been collected by a third party, for example, government surveys. Your role will be to interpret this information. Most desk research can be carried out literally fom one's desk using a phone, modem or fax, but occasionally a visit to a library will be required.

D'YOU MIND IF I ASK YOU A FEW QUESTIONS...

Many marketing problems can be solved quite simply through the use of published information and these secondary sources can provide highly diverse data, which are often surprisingly cheap to obtain. Of course, the real problem is knowing where to find them.

If the information is good it might provide a complete solution but, even if it is incomplete, it will generally enable certain information gaps to be closed. In addition it might suggest a suitable methodology for the primary research to follow.

Secondary research benefits

- Cheap
- Avoids repeating effort
- Quick to obtain
- Enables cost effective analysis of several data sources
- Easier to establish trends
- Can preserve complete confidentiality

Secondary research problems

- Research has not been published on your area of interest
- Often the information is more than two years old
- The information will be too general for complex problems
- There is little control over the quality of information.

What relevant published sources of information can you think of for your own business? Make a list and add to it as we go through the sources listed below.

Internal sources

Sales reports
Potentially a most useful source of information but often underused. In many organisations the sales report is used only as a means of control or of performance measurement, whereas its scope could be much wider.

The sales force is one of the few arms of a company that has direct contact with the market place. It is in an excellent position to provide a wide range of information, on competitor activity, new product potential, for example, or on improvements that could be made to existing products.

Sales reports can easily be extended to include information that will add to your company's overall understanding of its market place.

Does your company produce the type of sales reports that can be used in this way? If not the sales force is being under-utilised. Suggest some changes and, depending on the type of problem you have been asked to solve, try talking to the sales department for their impressions – you might be surprised.

Sales records will also give information on customer distribution and frequency of purchase etc. More importantly, sales records can be used to assess the impact of promotional support, for example, the effectiveness of an advertising campaign can be measured by any corresponding increase in sales.

This is especially true today with the rapid development of Electronic Point of Sale (EPOS)systems. These record sales at local outlets and relay them back to a central office for interpretation and action. The sensitivity and speed of EPOS systems can give the product manager immediate feedback at local, regional or national level.

Public relations department
Public relations records will include information pertinent to potential projects. A scan of PR records might provide information concerning perceived product quality (from customer complaints); it might provide leads on new product potential; it might also identify problems in distribution from enquiries such as, 'Where can I buy Whammo? My mother swears by it, but I've looked every-where in my town and can't find it.'

The PR department is the 'face' of the company. It spends most of its time persuading or explaining or just smiling. But it can also look and listen. Like the sales department, it is in contact with the market place. Used well it can provide important marketing intelligence.

Previously commissioned research
This might sound simple, but are you sure that another department hasn't carried out research into the same or similar problems? A quick check of relevant departments might save you an enormous amount of time and money, not to mention embarrassment, when you present the results of your expensive survey to an audience already familiar with the answers.

Management accounts
Management accounts will provide overall information on the company's financial performance as well as more specific information on product or sector profitability. They form an indispensable tool in the internal management of the company and as such provide a starting point for the comparative analysis of your competitors' activities.

Management accounts provide decision support and, as such, have an integral role in the planning of research projects.

In order to gain full benefit from the work your own company's management accountant does and to be able to compare internal accounts with your competitors, you should have some knowledge of the interpretation of accounts.

Personnel
Where have your colleagues been all their lives? If your task involves competitor analysis there is a chance that

somebody in your company will have worked with the subject of your enquiry. Check with personnel and if necessary, debrief the staff involved.

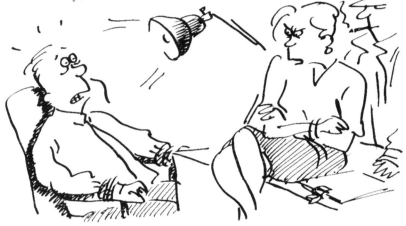

Other departments
Other departments might well hold information pertinent to the research problem. Purchasing departments, production and, of course, marketing should all have a store of accessible information that will often provide the basis of a solution to a research problem.

Internal sources checklist:

- Sales reports
- Public relations
- Previously commissioned research
- Management accounts
- Personnel
- Other departments.

External sources inside the UK

Government sources
Official statistics produced by the government can provide good, and often free, information for the researcher. These range from social trends reported in the census of population to economic activity as recorded in, for example, overseas trade statistics and specific business monitors.

Whilst much of this information can still only be obtained by personal visit, there are moves to bring some of the more popular sources on-line. The scope of the coverage of the economic and social life of the nation in these publications is substantial and space does not permit a full exposition here.

A list of government publications is available from:

Central Statistical Office,
Information Services Department, Room 58/G,
Government Offices, Great George St,
London SW1P 3AQ

Key government publications

- Social trends
- Economic trends
- Monthly Digest of Statistics
- Census reports
- Overseas trade statistics
- Family Expenditure Survey
- Retail price indices

Financial information on companies is available from:

Companies House,
65–71 City Road,
London EC1Y 1BB

This holds copies of the accounts of all private limited and public limited companies, and all limited partnerships.

Limited companies still trading must produce and file:

- A directors' report reviewing business development
- A profit and loss account
- A balance sheet
- Notes to the accounts
- The auditor's report

Copies of these can be inspected and are available on personal application. A number of private companies will also provide accounts for a fee.

Trade associations and regulatory bodies
If your industry has an association looking after its interests, then part of its remit might be to provide information to member companies. The Brewers' Society, for example, produces an annual report giving a full exposition on the national brewing industry and also provides data on international markets.

Trade associations will generally provide these reports to non-members and the secretaries or research staff of trade bodies may be a fount of information on their industry. A directory of UK and European trade bodies is available from:

CBD Research Ltd,
15 Wickham Road,
Beckenham,
Kent BR3 2JS

This directory covers all the trade associations in Great
Britain and they range from the Road Surface Dressing
Association to the British Chicken Information Service.
There is sure to be some form of association dealing with
your area of enquiry.

As well as trade associations, regulatory bodies such as
Oftel, Fimbra and the Chartered Institutes will have
information on their areas of interest. They are all worth a
try.

Pressure groups
Organisations concerned about various aspects of
commercial life might have information departments that
gather and disseminate information as part of their
activities. Friends of the Earth, for example, might provide
information on environmental standards and product
recycling laws.

Commercial sources
There is a wide range of commercial organisations which
publish data on a multi-client basis on almost every aspect
of marketing research.

The Henley Centre: one amongst a number of organisations
providing social and economic data and forecasts which can
be used to form an analysis of the marketing environment.
Mintel, The Economist Intelligence Unit, ERC: numerous
companies produce regular syndicated reports on a wide
range of market sectors. Many of these reports are held in
libraries, for example, the City Business Library in London.
A list of recently published syndicated reports is available
from the Chartered Institute of Marketing whose own
library contains some of the reports.
MEAL Ltd: produces regular information on advertising
expenditure by product, by media. This can be used to track
the advertising expenditure of competitors and, in tandem
with other key information, for example, market share data,
can also be used to assess the overall effectiveness of any
campaign.
A.C. Nielsen: provides audit data to create highly detailed
analyses of market shares and market size. *AGB* does a
similar job using a panel of consumers and a consumption
diary.
Kompass: provides directories of companies listed by
industry, product range, location and name. Kompass is
useful for establishing the broadest range of players in any
particular market sector. Contact names and numbers are
also recorded.

Lists of market research companies and their activities,
along with management consultancies who can carry out

desk research for you, are available from the Market Research Society, The Chartered Institute of Marketing or from several directories, for example, the European Management Index published by:

Project 1992 Ltd,
7–11 Kensington High Street,
London W8 5NP

Most industries have a specialised trade magazine devoted to them. If research is to be undertaken on a continuous basis, then a subscription is a good idea. For more specific, ad hoc studies, order back copies containing any relevant articles. Trade and other magazines are listed in:

The Advertisers Annual,
Reed Information Services,
East Grinstead,
West Sussex RH19 1XA

Conversations with the journalists working in various sectors of industry can be rewarding both in terms of information gleaned and further contacts recommended.

For information on, say, the biscuit market you could also look at food ingredients or capital equipment trade magazines. Think around the subject and results will come.

The local and national press and general interest magazines can also be useful. Try local press for detailed information on competitors at local level. News of capital investment, lay-offs or industrial unrest might make the local paper but fail to reach the national press.

On-line services
On-line data bases now cover almost every aspect of marketing research. Some are industry specific, for example,

Leatherhead Food Association's 'Foodline.' Others are more general, for example, Reuters' 'Textline'. They range from cheap to very expensive and the level of fee usually depends on the quality of information contained within them, although not always.

To save money, it is important to gain a thorough training in the most efficient use of on-line time.

If regular use is to be made of any particular service then it is often possible to negotiate an annual one-off fee. You will need to assess how often you will use the service.

Directories of on-line services are obtainable from any large public library. Central libraries often have subscriptions to certain on-line services and for a fee, will undertake specific searches.

Company publications
The information a company publishes about itself can furnish the researcher with a great deal of information:

- The annual report
- Information packs, careers advice etc
- Product brochures and price lists
- The company newspaper
- Company market reviews
- Press releases

External sources outside the UK

Many research tasks now have a European or international aspect. European research is currently the fastest growing area of the market research industry.

Obviously, a number of different factors come into play in conducting international desk research, such as:

* Language skills: are you able to translate sources?
* Budget: every aspect of research from faxing to commissioning becomes more expensive
* Time zones: at lunch, asleep or wrong number?
* Holidays: Europe closes in August
* Communications: problems with phone lines.
* Access to libraries: does the budget allow travel?
* Unreliable, or lack of, official sources

These difficulties should not put you off. A large number of English language sources are available but if you have a foreign language so much the better but you can often find someone in an organisation who speaks English.

In addition the marketing services industry has expanded to take in the opportunity presented to it by the Europeanisation of English businesses. Try the European Management Index for companies who have the expertise and capacity to carry out work internationally.

Many of the sources applicable to UK research apply equally to Europe and indeed worldwide. A knowledge of sources means many international markets can be well researched.

Sources which are specifically international include:

- United Nations Data, for example, Food and Agriculture organisation
- Statistical reports of the EEC, EFTA, and Benelux; Eurostat
- UK Chambers of Commerce abroad
- International banks
- International research companies/consultancies
- The OECD
- Parastatal organisations, for example, the WHO
- The annual reports of multinational companies
- The DTI export information service
- International trade associations

Many other overseas sources are listed in:

The European Directory of Marketing Information Sources,
Euromonitor Publications Ltd,
87–88 Turnmill Street,
London EC1M 5QU

Summary

Today we have reviewed the variety of published sources that are available to enable effective answers to many marketing problems. The use of secondary sources can be extremely cost efficient.

You should now be able to produce a comprehensive list of secondary sources for your own business.

Tomorrow we will take a look at primary research and the techniques involved in carrying it out.

Primary research techniques

Secondary sources may answer the objectives identified in our brief. If not then at least we should have a much better idea of the information gaps that will need to be filled through primary research. Today we shall begin to look at primary research techniques and will examine:

- Qualitative and quantitative research
- Observation
- Experimentation
- Survey research

Qualitative and quantitative research

Very often these two terms are presented as if they were two extremes. Of course they are very different but should be seen as complementary methodologies. The best research designs will use a mix to improve the results of the project.

Qualitative research
The information gathered is generally impossible to justify statistically but conveys feeling or insight. Results are based on a small sample, maybe no more than twenty to thirty people. The key technique used is observation. The emphasis is placed on opinion and meaning and it looks at why and how things happen.

The sample will generally be far too small to make valid assumptions about the feelings of the entire target group.

Qualitative research can, however, provide crucial information, which can then be explored further through quantitative work.

Qualitative information is used to:

- Clarify issues prior to quantitative studies
- Identify possible new product development
- Assess consumer perceptions of products or competitors
- Generate hypotheses
- Analyse consumer behaviour
- Examine how purchase decisions are made
- Establish the emotional reasons why a brand is preferred

Quantitative research
This is statistically based and is the better known currency of market research. It examines how much, who, where and when. This is the type of research that gives us the state of

the political parties in the opinion polls. It uses the techniques of sampling, questionnaires, and computer based data processing to produce valid quantitative estimates.

It is more time consuming than qualitative work and more expensive but is important if our problem has a quantitative aspect, for example when deciding future output levels.

Quantitative information is used to:

• Establish the rate of use of a product or service, for example, to establish how many people of a certain social class buy a product or service
• Indicate preferences, for example, to establish brand shares
• Support decisions with a quantitative aspect

Research techniques

As we have indicated, there are three different techniques available to enable us to collect both qualitative and quantitative information. These are observation, experimentation and survey research.

To obtain the best results it is useful to use a mix of different techniques. Combining techniques can:

• Help to reduce bias
• Reveal errors in measurement
• Verify and cross check data
• Increase response rates

Another requirement for the production of good research is a scientific approach. Information, as we have said, needs to be accurate, timely and pertinent. In order to ensure the decisions made are based on the best information available to us we should try for an approach to problem solving which:

- Is objective and unbiased
- Produces conclusions based on results
- Tests our opinions
- Confirms or alters our preconceptions

Observational research
Many researchers have found that the best results are obtained through the use of observational techniques. The main advantage is that they generally catch the subject off guard. People tend to stiffen when confronted with a questionnaire.

The very act of reaction to an external stimulus like a questionnaire can induce an element of bias into our research. If the observed person is unaware of our presence the effect of reaction is removed, although there are still questions which need to be answered:

- What is the effect of our observation on the subject?
- As observers do we only see what we want to see?
- How do we effectively record results?
- Are we making assumptions?
- How do we find skilled observers?

The advantages however are substantial and, perhaps the main benefit is that, we can see the target of our research in its natural environment.

Techniques of observational research include:

Concealed recording equipment, especially video. For example, a recent study used video cameras hidden inside television sets to record the audiences exposure and attention to advertisements;

Participant observation: the observer plays a role and records results derived from interaction with the target group;
Non-participatory observation: the researcher adopts a passive role, recording actions or comments from the target group;
Unobtrusive methods: no direct contact is made with the target of the research. For example, examining the amount of litter on the floor of a cinema to see how much was bought before the film.
Panel data: perhaps the best known observational method. These are used to determine things like shopping behaviour, food consumption patterns and audience viewing figures.

The key techniques used for collecting panel data are:

Consumption diaries: the members of the panel record all purchases in a shopping diary. Analysis of the data can give the size of the market, brand shares within the market and data on the impact of special offers etc. The advent of bar coding has led to increasing accuracy. Members of the panel are given a bar code reader which they use to record purchases. Audits of Great Britain (AGB) is perhaps the best known supplier of this type of panel based data;
Audits: A.C. Nielsen Co. Ltd is perhaps the best known supplier of retail audit data in the world. Its system works on the simple assumption that the the sales of any item in any store over a month can be worked out using the following equation:

Stocks at the beginning of the month
plus Purchases by the store during the month
less Stocks held at the end of the month
equals Sales

Observation is a central method in market research and has several advantages.

Advantages of observation checklist

- The subject of the research is in a natural environment
- It identifies areas for in-depth or quantitative research
- It can help frame problems in unfamiliar areas
- It avoids problems of poor expression or understanding
- It can be a lot more accurate than survey research
- It avoids problems of recall
- Management can keep in touch with the market place

To be effective, observation must:

- Use skilled observers
- Use standardised recording methods
- Take place at a representative time and place
- Be combined with other methods

Experimentation

This is the only way of verifying cause and effect in the marketing of goods and services. It is not an ideal method as in the real world consumers are subject to many influences.

What we try to do in market research experiments is to:

- Assess what factors influence any action
- Discover what the key factors are
- Establish how much influence they have

The researcher must be able to:

- Control the relative impact of these factors
- Limit the effect of uncontrollable factors, such as the weather

All these different factors can be put into different categories:

- Primary factors: where a change in behaviour is directly caused by a change in controllable influences on the market, for example, a price reduction causes an increase in sales;
- Secondary factors: change is caused by an uncontrolled factor, for example, bad summers cause ice cream sales to fall;
- Error factors: the wrong factors causing the change are identified. There are ways to avoid this costly error. The use of controls can help. For example, we could

measure the effectiveness of an advertising campaign by measuring the changes in sales levels in one area and comparing them against an area where the campaign has not been run.

Test marketing is an important experimental technique. This involves the launch or test of a new product or service at a local level prior to an extended or national launch. A launch at a local level can help iron out problems before a substantial amount of money is invested.

Survey Research
This area of research is undoubtedly the best known field of market research. So much so that inexperienced researchers use this method as their main method of gathering information. It involves the process of obtaining data through questions.

We have already seen that the other methods outlined above might be more appropriate to certain research solutions and that certainly a mix of methods is better still.

It is possible to identify three broad types of market research survey. These are defined by the use to which the results are put.

Surveys are used for:
- Establishing facts
- Finding opinions
- Interpreting actions or opinions

Establishing facts: these surveys are designed to establish patterns of behaviour. The information generated is hard and gives quantified statistics on, for example, usage and behaviour. Typical questions would be:

- Do you have a car?
- When did you last buy a car?
- What make was it?
- What was the engine size?
- Where did you buy it?
- How often do you use it?

We can also establish details of the size of our market, which could be overall, by brand , by segment or by sales outlet, and we can find details of usage occasion;

Finding opinions: designed to discover attitudes, beliefs, and awareness. It is soft data but can provide information to help frame advertising copy or suggest areas for new product development. A typical question would be: Can you describe the feel of the car?

Interpreting actions or opinions: here we are trying to establish the motivations behind beliefs and actions. Typical questions would be:

- Why do you use a car as opposed to the train?
- Why does this car make you feel this way?
- Why did you buy this model as opposed to another?

The responses are likely to vary considerably and will be difficult to analyse. Data tends to be of a more qualitative nature and the interpretation is subjective.

Work out a list of questions for the above types of survey research for your own product or service.

Checklist of survey research benefits:

- It provides information on a wide population relatively cheaply
- It can fill a wide range of information needs
- It is relatively efficient and flexible

Checklist of survey research problems:

- Bias
- Lack of understanding or misconceptions
- Misinformation
- Non-response

Summary

Today we have introduced the techniques of primary research.

We have shown that primary research can generate a wide range of information but it is usually qualitative or quantitative.

We saw that qualitative work usually precedes quantitative.

We have seen that the research methodology selected will depend on the nature of the problem to be solved and that a problem that is expressed in quantitative terms will generally be solved through the use of quantitative techniques.

We looked at the three types of primary research: observation, experimentation and survey. We saw that, whilst each has its merits, the best solutions involve a mixture of these methods.

We also saw that survey research has many advantages but that the issues addressed by survey research are often derived from prior use of the other techniques.

Tomorrow we shall look more closely at the methods available to help us gather our information. These include: sampling, and the design and administration of questionnaires.

Primary research in practice

Today we shall look at the practical aspects of primary research. These are:

- Sampling
- Questionnaires
- Types of question
- Piloting

Sampling

Surveys can be as large as we wish. Technically, we could question everybody who will influence or be affected by our decision. This is known as our survey universe or population.

Occasionally, the entire survey population will need to be surveyed. This is known as a census. However, we have seen that survey research is expensive and in most surveys interviewing every member of our universe is impractical.

Populations of interest to us may be well defined already. For example, we may only be interested in people under a certain age, but even narrowly defined populations might still be too large to survey.

Sampling allows us to obtain valid data on a small section of a population. From this we can draw valid conclusions about the population as a whole.

The main sampling methods used in market research are:

- Random or probability sampling
- Quota or non-probability sampling

Accuracy depends on a close definition of our chosen population. This definition is known as the sample frame. Commonly, the electoral register has been used as the basis for identifying adults over 18. The frame could also be a measure of location, for example, all those living in a certain region. The sample frame defines our survey population. There are also a growing number of lists commercially available that might be used to narrow our sample frame.

Checklist for a good sample frame

- Accurate, with no duplication
- Complete
- Up to date
- Relevant to the objectives of the survey
- Accessible

Within the sample frame we can specify sample units, that is, the members of the frame we wish to interview based on age, sex, lifestyle etc. Think of the direct mail you receive; why have you been chosen?

Random or probability sampling

This means that each member of the sample frame has an equal chance of being selected. The advantages of random sampling lie in the fact that we can establish the statistical validity of our sample and the accuracy of our data.

We have all seen opinion polls which give the state of the political parties. Survey results are described as subject to a margin of error of ±3%. Establishing the voting intentions of the country by interviewing 1,500 people can only yield approximate results. Larger samples mean more accurate results and reduce margins of error.

It is important to be sure that the sample is sound. We do this by comparing the sample with the overall population from which it is taken. Through this we can give a level of confidence. This might indicate that the sample is correct to a confidence of 95%. This means there is a 20/1 chance of our sample being unrepresentative. Market research projects usually work at a 95% confidence level.

Limits of accuracy and confidence levels can be decided before the survey. The levels at which they are set will depend on the type of decision made. The more important the decision, the greater the levels of confidence required. For a greater degree of accuracy and confidence, a larger sample will be surveyed. Of course, this means the survey will be more expensive.

Once confidence requirements and accuracy limits are decided, we can establish the number of interviews needed to provide figures to these specifications.

Quota or non-probability sampling
Often samples are based on a subjective decision of what is a representative sample. Quota sampling goes some way to balancing subjectivity by comparing our sample with characteristics displayed in the population as a whole.

Problems lie in the fact that although some characteristics may be easily identified and distributed, others may not. For example, it is easy to stratify by age or sex but difficult to produce quotas by lifestyle.

This method is also more subjective because the research team will decide on the population characteristics used to establish quotas.

The advantages of quota sampling are cost and speed.It avoids the problem of establishing a sophisticated sample frame. Interviewers do not have to contact all specified individuals but only those that fall within the predefined quotas.

Questionnaires

The questionnaire is an important tool in market research. It can provide information on the following:

- Facts
- Opinions
- Motives
- Behaviour

We use questionnaires for several reasons:

- We need to collect and record data
- We need comparable data
- We need to ask questions in the same way to minimise bias

A great deal of work can be put into the background to a research project. This can be wasted if the questionnaire is not right.

SO WHAT WAS THE KEY MOTIVATOR BEHIND YOUR PURCHASE?

So what makes a good questionnaire? Well, it must be:

- Understandable and unambiguous
- Focused and relevant to the problem
- Simple for both interviewers and processors to use.

There are several key issues to be addressed when writing a questionnaire.

Make sure that the question is understandable: questionnaires should use everyday language that is simple to understand.
Questions must be unambiguous: narrow the terms of reference down as much as possible. Terms of frequency and time should be specified. Questions like 'how often do you travel by bus?' are not clear; 'often' can mean different things to different people;
Avoid leading the respondent: many questions can be unconsciously loaded to create a desired response. A question like 'most people believe that this brand is better, do you?' is an obvious example. People will follow the crowd.
Avoid embarrassing questions: questions on income, personal behaviour etc. should be avoided or left until the end of the interview. A skilled interviewer can establish a rapport with the respondent which will make it easier to gain a satisfactory response.
Use economy of expression: break down complex sentences and use simple phrases.
Never overestimate intelligence: the questions should be capable of being understood by the least educated member of the sample. Similarly do not overstretch the respondent's memory.

Be careful of questions relating to personal status or pride: in one instance, the job description, waste management artisan, was recorded by an interviewer as a management position. In fact, the respondent was a dustman.

It is well known by doctors that levels of smoking or drinking are usually understated.

Use showcards only when really necessary: chosen by the researcher they can induce bias.

On a more practical level:

- An introduction to the questionnaire will help to secure attention
- An incentive for completion can also be given
- Use a clear type face and reasonable quality paper
- Spread the questionnaire out as far as possible
- Leave room for coding the answers
- Only ask questions relevant to survey objectives
- Distinguish interviewer instructions; italics or emboldening will help the interviewer to work efficiently

Take care over question order: the order in which questions are posed can have a bearing on the responses given. This is a key weakness of omnibus surveys.

Question sequence: this should also be looked at carefully. There are usually defined sections to a questionnaire and they take the following order:

Interview identification: includes the number of the interview, the interviewer, the time, date and location.

Introduction: this may include the interviewer presenting some form of official identification and a general outline of the broad use of the survey.

The main body of the questionnaire: this will cover the questions related to the objectives of the survey. Opening questions should be designed to stimulate interest. They will include questions which filter out respondents, related perhaps to levels of usage of our product or service. If respondents are not regular users then we can possibly skip sections of the questionnaire. Following questions should take the respondent systematically through the questionnaire.

Classification data: if we are conducting a quota survey then these questions should be asked before the main body of the questionnaire. Otherwise it is best to leave them to the end of the survey. Data collected will relate to age, sex, income, education etc. We might also want the respondent's name and address to allow us to carry out random checks of the interviews. Again this is better left to the end of the questionnaire.

Types of question

There are two basic question types:

- Closed
- Open-ended

Closed questions
These offer the respondent a choice of answers and may be simple yes/no questions or multiple choice. With multiple choice, take care over the choice of answers; piloting can indicate unexpected responses.

Closed questions also include the use of scales. We can use scales to measure qualitative attitudes to a product or service. The most commonly used are:

The Likert scale: our sample is given a statement and asked how much they agree or disagree. The answers are recorded on a five point scale and the results can be combined to give an average score.

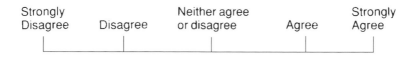

Semantic differential: this is useful in establishing the perceived image of a product or service. Respondents are asked to describe the object of the survey in terms of its position on a seven point scale within two opposite words or phrases. For example:

Good – Bad
Efficient – Inefficient
Easy to use – Hard to use
Fashionable – Unfashionable

Importance scale: this is used to describe product features along a scale of importance. It is useful for assessing product development opportunities.

Verbal frequency: respondents may be unable to give precise information on how often they act or behave in a certain way, for example, to specify how many times a year they buy soft drinks. However, we would like to establish who are the heaviest users of our product. Using verbal frequency will provide a broad idea. Respondents rank behaviour on the following scale:

| Never | Seldom | Sometimes | Often | Always |

Scales are particularly useful in qualitative research. They can be used to explain and predict behaviour and can yield key supplementary information for our quantitative work.

Open- ended questions
These can be of several types:

- Unstructured: a completely free response is recorded;
- Sentence completion: I would buy whammo because...
- Word association: respondents are asked to respond to prompts with the first word they think of;
- Story completion: respondents are asked to complete a brief scenario about various aspects of our product.

The advantages of open-ended questions lie in the removal of bias. Problems lie in the recording of long replies.

Piloting

It is essential to test the questionnaire. This can reveal problems in question phrasing and layout. Look for:

- Respondents' understanding
- Difficulty in answering
- Problems in questions order
- Respondent interest and attention span
- Effectiveness of filter and skip questions
- Ease of coding and analysis

Piloting can also help develop our feel for the problem overall and enable us to add or delete questions. It can add to the quality of the research overall.

Piloting will only add a little in proportion to the total cost of the survey, but should enhance effectiveness. It can also save a lot of money.

GOOD PILOT!

Summary

Today we looked at the practical aspects of carrying out a research survey. We saw the advantages of sampling and discussed the several methods available to enable us to create a valid sample. In short, we have to decide:

- Who to survey
- How many to survey
- How to choose them

We have seen two different methods for selecting a sample.

We also looked at the questionnaire and stressed the importance of:

- Comprehension
- Brevity
- Clarity
- Design
- Piloting

We finished by looking at open-ended and closed questions and the usefulness of scales to measure attitudes.

Tomorrow we will look at carrying out the survey and how we go about analysing the results.

Surveys and data analysis

Today, we will examine how a survey is administered and analysed. We will look at:

- Types of interview
- Interviewers
- Carrying out the interview
- Other data collection methods
- Editing, coding and processing
- Data analysis

Types of interview

Selection of the interview technique will depend on the nature of the research task we have been asked to solve. The basic types of interview are:

- Structured
- Semi-structured
- Unstructured

Structured Interviews
The interviewer administers a questionnaire and must stick to it. There is little scope for interviewer initiative. Questions are closed and respondents cannot add anything that is not in the questionnaire.

Advantages	Disadvantages
• Quick to complete	• Inflexible
• Low cost	• Limited information
• Low skill factor	• Potential for bias
• Ease of processing	

Semi-structured interviews
A combination of closed and open-ended questions, which gives more flexibility. There is still a formal structure but more room is given for the response. Interviewers might be instructed to 'probe' for more information.

Advantages	Disadvantages
• Quantitative and qualitative information can be gathered	• Higher skill factor
• Respondent interest is greater	• Problems recording response
• Complex information	• Higher cost

Unstructured interviews
There are two types of unstuctured interview:

- Depth interviews
- Group discussions

Depth interviews: the aim is to uncover the real motivations behind actions and discover why attitudes are held. The interviewer encourages the respondent to answer questions as fully as possible but involvement is kept to a minimum. Interviews may last for over an hour. The technique demands the use of a specialist; often psychiatrists are used. Results are recorded on video or on tape.

Advantages	Disadvantages
• Identify ideas and hypotheses	• Cost
• Supports quantitative work	• Specialists needed
• Provides feeling and insight	

Group discussions: these will always produce qualitative data. The group will normally be made up of 8–12 members. Members are chosen because they have a knowledge of the subject under discussion. For example, they might all be regular users of our product. They will all generally be of a similar background. The interviewers role is to guide the discussion and to stimulate the interaction of the group. The discussions are taped.

Advantages	Disadvantages
• Comprehension is easier	• Opinion leaders influence
• Flexibility	
• A wider range of response	• Lack of control
• Group comfort and stimulation	• Levelling of response
• Respondents use everyday language	• Need for skilled moderators
• Cost	
• Speed	

The technique can provide information on motivation. It can generate new product ideas or help identify deficiencies in our current product. It can help narrow our terms of reference.

When carrying out group work, we should consider the venue carefully. The discussion should have some broad objectives within which the moderator has to work. A skilled moderator can produce very useful results from a good group.

Interviewers

The quality of the field workers is obviously crucial to the outcome of the research. But how do we ensure the quality of the field staff carrying out our survey? The answer is by carefully:

- Selecting and training staff
- Briefing them
- Controlling them

Selecting and training staff
As we have seen, the skills required by our interviewers will vary according to the type of survey. Some companies do keep their own interviewers but it is more practical for most to use a specialised field work agency. Research agencies will have their own panel of interviewers.

Checklist for appointing our own staff

- The ability to listen
- Mobility
- A nondescript social background
- A reasonable education, literacy and numeracy to GCSE level
- Past experience in research or people oriented work

Checklist for appointing an agency

- Their experience in relevant research techniques
- Size and experience of the field force
- Selection procedures
- Training methods
- Interviewer motivation
    - how are they paid, hourly or per interview?
    - are they permanent staff?
- The quality of field supervisors and managers
- Membership of a professional body or interviewer scheme

Briefing

All interviewers must be adequately instructed on the background and objectives of the research project, the sampling procedure (how the data is to be recorded and the number of interviews to be carried out and by when), and given instruction on the time, place and date of the interviews.

Control

We must ensure that researchers are carrying out the work properly.

Checklist for controlling staff

- What checks are made on interviewers in the field?
- How do interviewers ask for help if there are problems?
- What is the ratio of supervisors to interviewers?
- Is the briefing carried out personally, by phone or by post?
- Is there a written reference guide?
- How often do supervisors see interviewers?
- Is interviewer performance monitored over time?
- What spot checks are made on the interviews?

Under the interviewer card scheme, a minimum of 5% of work should be checked within 24 hours and any doubts should be followed up by a 100% check.

Carrying out the interview

Checklist of basic rules

- Always introduce the questionnaire
- Stick exactly to the wording and order of the questions
- Do not elaborate or explain the question
- Always follow the set procedure for the question
- Try to avoid non-response

Things to consider

Filter questions: these will take respondents more easily through the questionnaire and they avoid asking unnecessary questions. They will include skip instructions. For example:

Do you smoke	Yes	☐	1
	No	☐	2

If No go to question 6

Probes and Prompts: these are intended to encourage the respondent:

- To say more in answer to an open question
- To explain an answer
- To answer the question

They should be used carefully as they can easily introduce bias. We must never put words into the respondent's mouth.

Show Cards: these are used to prompt an answer:

- Always show rather than explain the cards in order
- Always ensure the answer given is one of the choices on the card
- Always read any question on the card

Other data collection methods

There are other ways of collecting data rather than face to face interviews. The main methods are:

- Postal surveys
- Telephone survey
- Call and collect
- Omnibus surveys

Postal or fax surveys
These surveys involve sending or handing out a questionnaire for self-completion. The survey is then mailed or faxed back for processing (if by post this is by means of a pre-paid envelope).

Advantages	Disadvantages
• Reach over a dispersed sample	• Low response (10% is common)
• Useful for industrial research	• Self-selection
• Completion is at respondent's convenience	• Depth of information
• Relatively cheap	• Speed
• Fax still has attention grabbing quality	

Telephone Surveys

87% of households have access to a telephone and this, combined with improved technology, has led to an increase in telephone research.

Computer-Assisted Telephone Interviewing (CATI) means that responses can be fed staight into computer which speeds processing. We could even use computer administered questionnaires.

We can also reach respondents that might be more difficult to contact for face to face interviews, for example chief executives.

Advantages	Disadvantages
• Control	• Problems with recall
• Speed of processing	• Resistance to phone interviewing
• Relatively cheap	
• Easy to check and follow up	
• Quick response to events	

Call and collect

Here the interviewer leaves the questionnaire and returns later to collect it. This has several advantages, in that the respondent can consider replies at length and any problems can be discussed with the interviewer on return. It is also slightly cheaper than the traditional face to face interview.

Omnibus surveys

Omnibus surveys combine the primary research requirements of several companies on one questionnaire. They are an important way of cutting the cost of primary market research. They can use the techniques of postal, telephone or face to face interviews and typically interview 1,000 to 2,000 respondents. Surveys are carried out weekly with results available eight days after interviewing.

Many companies are represented on the survey and this is its key disadvantage. Our question could be one of hundreds on many different subjects. This can introduce bias. They are, however, very cheap with a low cost per interview. They also cut the time involved in working out samples, appointing agencies etc. They can be very useful if a decision to be taken will have marginal return.

An example of an omnibus survey is the BMRB's weekly access survey.

Editing, coding and processing

Once the questionnaire is complete it must be prepared for analysis. First it must be checked. It is important work. We must ensure:

- Each question been completed
- Answers are accurate and consistent
- The respondent is part of the desired sample

If there are any doubts, call-backs can be made to respondents and the information checked or added to. It should be stressed that well trained and well briefed interviewers can save a great deal of time at this stage of the survey.

Editing
Editing can be carried out manually or by a computer which is programmed to check for ommissions or inconsistencies.

Coding
After editing we can code the responses. The object of coding is to give each answer a number which can then be processed by computer.

Many quantitative questions can be pre-coded and they can be completed by the interviewer as the answer is given. Coding space is usually on the right hand side of the questionnaire.

Open-ended responses must be analysed and each different response given a number. We do not have to look at all questionnaires: 10% should cover most responses.

CATI obviously avoids this stage of the process as data is fed into the computer straight away.

Processing
The object is to produce a consistent set of data which can then be read for analysis. This can be done by:

Punchcards: a question is allocated one or more of 80 columns with 12 rows. The various coded answers are punched into the card. Cards should be checked. The cards are then sorted and tabulated by a machine

Computers: the information is typed directly into a programmed computer and tabulated and analysed. There is custom software available for the analysis of surveys, for example, SPSS (Statistical Package for the Social Sciences). This area is developing rapidly. Optical character recognition, for example, avoids the errors possible with manual input.

Smaller surveys could be processed by hand which is generally cheaper, and quicker for simple analyses.

Data Analysis

Processed data is presented as a series of tables. These will show the number of respondents who gave a particular answer to a particular question. Tables will be provided for the sample as a whole and for sub-samples, for example, by sex or age. We can also generate cross-tabulation. This compares the answers to more than one question.

It is important to generate usable data. It is easy to ask for too many tables. The majority of tables are left unused. Stick to the objectives of the research and follow the plan.

Data can be analysed using several techniques. These include the simple techniques of averages, data range, frequency (the mode) and mid-point (median) or more technical analytical tools.

We should, however, only use techniques that match objectives. We should move through the various stages of analysis to help our understanding of relationships within the data. Our research department or agency will help us with the more sophisticated techniques that can be used.

In practice, most major decisions can be supported by simple methods. If we need powerful statistical tools to find relationships, will they be capable of supporting profitable business decisions?

Checklist of important considerations in data analysis:

- Do not be a slave to technique: select the appropriate technique for the task in hand;
- Analysis provides the basis for decisions: technical skill is no replacement for management experience and judgement
- Results must be understood even if sophisticated research techniques have been used
- Use a mix of analytical techniques
- Remember that the results are only as good as the data from which they are obtained
- Ensure that statistical results have a basis in reality
- Keep your eyes on the objectives of the research plan
- Learn to interpret statistics. Look for:
  - what is typical
  - significant differences
  - significant relationships

Summary

Today, we looked at how our data is gathered, processed and analysed. We saw that the research we produce is only as good as its weakest link. Interviewers have a significant role to play in ensuring the data is of a high quality.

We saw the importance of employing well-trained interviewers and that it is important to provide a good briefing. We also discussed the attributes of a good interviewer and looked at methods of control in the field.

We saw that, ultimately, answers given will be edited and coded to produce a set of numbers that can be analysed by hand or by machine.

Finally we introduced the range of analytical tools available to us. These help manipulate the data to enable telling interpretations to be made. It is on the interpretation of the data that management will base decisions.

Tomorrow we will look at the presentation of data in the final report.

The final report

Over the past six days we have seen how a market research plan is conceived and executed. Key to the success of the project, however, is the communication of its findings.

These findings can be presented through the means of a personal presentation or written report. Generally, a combination of these methods is used. However, the key to a successful research project is the written report. This will be referred to long after the most dazzling of personal presentations is forgotten.

So today we will look at the following:

- Personal presentation
- Report structure and content
- What makes a good report

Personal presentation

A personal presentation of the results of market research projects is often useful. It should cement the close working relationship, that has hopefully been built up during the course of a project, between the manager of the project and the agency, department or person carrying out the project.

From the project manager's point of view, a personal presentation can enable a closer 'feel' for the written report. For maximum benefit, the written report should have been presented before the date of the oral presentation.

The personal presentation should not be viewed as a confrontation but rather as a meeting of minds. Any problems with the written report should be notified to the researcher prior to the personal meeting, especially if they are of a technical or involved nature.

From the researcher's viewpoint, the personal presentation can be nerve wracking but it certainly focuses the mind on what might be picked on as the weaker areas of the written report.

Personal presentation is a skill in itself but for the researcher, the task should not be difficult. The researcher should know more by now about the problem and its potential solution than the audience. The research, if successfully conceived and executed, should reveal a solution to the research problem posed.

It is vital for a successful research presentation to focus on the solution to the problem rather than the methodology used to solve it. Ultimately, it is the key findings of the research and proposed solutions to problems that are of interest to the manager, not the innovative techniques used to establish them.

From the practical point of view, however, it is best to keep the formal part of any personal presentation as brief as possible. The attention span of any audience is limited as is one person's ability to sustain performance over more than perhaps one hour.

Enhance the effect of your presentation with the use of visual aids. If the research has been carried out by a team, divide the presentation between them.

Finally, leave time for a discussion. Here the main points can be developed and further supplementary research can be discussed by both sides.

Plan, prepare and practice your presentation. Don't let a poor personal performance over one hour detract from the vast amount of work that might have been put into the written report.

Six steps to successful personal presentations

- Focus on problem solving
- Keep it brief
- Keep it interesting
- Prepare and rehearse
- Leave good time for discussion
- Follow the client's brief

Report structure and content

The content of the report will be broadly dictated by the research plan developed to tackle a given problem. It will include:

- Problem definition and research objectives
- Research methodology
  - data collection
  - data analysis
- Recommendations and conclusions

The organisation of these various elements of the research plan within the structure of the report can vary. The overall structure will depend on the nature of the audience and the objectives of the report.

In the United Kingdom, the Market Research Society's code of practice gives guidelines as to what should be included in the final report. Of course, the full details of what should be included within the body of the written report, should be finalised in the briefing discussion between the researcher and the commissioner of the research.

Many companies who regularly commission research, release guidelines to suppliers which will cover the proposed structure of the report.

In some cases they will even give the standard colour of paper to be used for the different sections of the report, the ideal length of each section and instructions for the precise layout of graphics and tables.

These broad guidelines, normally issued to all agencies submitting proposals for research projects, will be refined and honed down following final appointment.

Generally the structure of a research report is as follows:

- Title page
- Contents page
- Introduction/objectives and scope
- Executive summary
- Research conclusions and interpretation of results
- Methodology
- Appendices
- Bibliography
- Glossary of terms
- Index

Title page

This should contain:
- A full description of the subject matter of the report
- The author's name (agency, department and contact number and/or address)
- Who the report has been prepared for
- Project or internal reference number and if it is a published report, any bibliographical information
- The date of presentation
- Any restricted access information

Contents page

This should contain a full list of the contents, including table titles and all main and sub-headings. Main headings can be distinguished by emboldening or numerical indication. The purpose should be to facilitate accessibility and the easy identification of report structure.

Introduction/objectives and scope

This should contain:
- The background to the problem; a brief case history
- Key factors that revealed the need for research
- Who commissioned the research
- The full objectives of the report
- The scope and the limits of the report
- Any exceptional considerations

S A T U R D A Y

Executive summary
This should present the essence of the report. It should not normally be more than three typed A4 pages.

The summary should summarise the objectives, the findings and if requested in the brief, the recommendations of the report. Points can be supported by references to the report's main body.

It is the keystone of a working document and represents the arguments upon which managers will base key decisions. For the researchers, it represents the fruits of their labour. Its importance cannot be underestimated.

Research conclusions and interpretation of results
This can be included where relevant as a supplement to the executive summary. It is particularly useful if the research is exploratory in its objectives, that is, the objectives do not dictate a definitive solution but rather an indication of potential. For example, a report on the trading conditions in a new overseas market. Normally it will add perhaps another two pages to the full report.

Methodology
Whilst the manager using the information might not be overly interested in the methodology used, the research manager of a commissioning company will need to assure the end user of a research project that a sound methodology has been used in its construction.

A technical appendix can further explore the intricacies of research methodology, but in the main body of the report we need an accessible description of questionnaire design, sampling techniques, sources used etc.

91

Key results, tables and graphs
The main function of this section of the report is to provide an exposition of those results that are directly relevant to the research brief.

The temptation is to include far too much detail. What is needed is the rifle approach rather than a process of saturation bombing.

These results should be supported graphically where possible. Remember, one diagram can say as much as several pages of text and, generally, diagrammatically presented information is far easier to assimilate.

Tables should be laid out so that the patterns they present and the information they contain is obvious at a glance. Indexing of numerical trends providing percentage breakdowns rounding of decimal places etc. are simple methods of making numerical data more accessible.

Within this section of the report we can flesh out findings by using already published facts, or previously commissioned research. It is important, however, that all new findings and conclusions can be supported by the research itself. The researcher or client must not bring their own preconceptions to the compilation or interpretation of the results.

Appendices
Generally, the appendices are the last major section of the report. Often they account for the majority of the report's volume and are composed of material not directly relevant to the understanding of the report. They should include the tools used to construct the report and the data underpinning its findings. They contain:

- A detailed description of sample design
- Copies of any questionnaires used, along with details of the field force and their briefing notes
- Full statistical tables as only extracts will have been included in the report up to now
- A full transcript of typical interviews, if in-depth interviews have been used
- Any supporting photographs or illustrations
- Correspondence

Bibliography

The bibliography is important if the research report is based around secondary sources, although adequate sourcing of tables and the use of footnotes can make this redundant. Secondary sources supporting primary research should also be listed.

Glossary

A glossary of terms is not always necessary but should be included if the audience is not specialist or if the subject area is unfamiliar. A technical subject might demand a detailed explanation of terms used. Research into foreign markets might also require an explanation of different definitions. If there is any room for doubt, include an explanation.

Index

Usually a contents page is sufficient but, if the client wants an index or the report is long, include it.

What makes a good report

We have looked at how a report should be put together and through this we should have some awareness of what makes good market research. If you are in management, there is a fair chance that you will read many more research reports than you will write. So how do we evaluate the quality of a report and what factors should we bear in mind when reading market research reports?

Consider:

- Who commissioned the report?
- Who conducted the research?
- Is the researcher a member of a professional body with a sound code of practice
- Is the research plan sound and appropriate?
    - is the sample fair?
    - is the plan controlled adequately?
    - are all technical details appended?

- – are details of analysis techniques given?
- – is there any allowance bias in the research design?
- Are data collection methods sound?
  - – is the field force adequately trained, motivated, briefed and controlled?
  - – is potential bias minimised here?
- Is the sample size adequate to support the conclusions made?
  - – are sampling error limits shown?
  - – is the sample reliable?
- Are the limits of the findings given?
- Are the assumptions behind the report's conclusions given?
- Is a full methodology given?
- Does it clearly present all relevant findings?
- Is it balanced and logical?
- Does it avoid jargon?
- Is it simple to read and accessible?

Summary

Today we looked at the presentation of the final report. We saw that it is an easy thing to spoil the most useful of research projects through poor presentation.

With careful planning and rehearsal and a positive approach from both sides, we saw the potential of the personal presentation of the research report.

The written report remains crucial. We saw that, if it is not to be left lying on a shelf, it must not only be soundly based technically but also well written and pitched at a level at which the intended audience will gain maximum benefit.

We have seen that the organisation of the contents of the report is key to providing a good working document that is accessible to the end user.

Finally we have established a set of criteria against which research quality can be measured.